The Odes of Solomon

Sacred Songs of Devotion and Divine Love

A Modern Translation

Adapted for the Contemporary Reader

King Solomon
(Early Christian Hymns)

Translated by Tim Zengerink

© **Copyright 2025**
All rights reserved.

It is not legal to reproduce, duplicate, or transmit any part of this document in either electronic means or in printed format. Recording of this publication is strictly prohibited and any storage of this document is not allowed unless with written permission from the publisher except for the use of brief quotations in a book review.

This book contains works of fiction. Any resemblance to persons living or dead, or places, events, or locations is purely coincidental.

Table Of Contents

Preface - Message to the Reader 1
Introduction 5
The Odes of Solomon 10
    Ode 1 11
    Ode 2 11
    Ode 3 11
    Ode 4 13
    Ode 5 14
    Ode 6 15
    Ode 7 16
    Ode 8 18
    Ode 9 20
    Ode 10 21
    Ode 11 22
    Ode 12 24
    Ode 13 26
    Ode 14 26
    Ode 15 27
    Ode 16 28
    Ode 17 29
    Ode 18 31
    Ode 19 32

Ode 20	33
Ode 21	34
Ode 22	35
Ode 23	36
Ode 24	38
Ode 25	39
Ode 26	40
Ode 27	41
Ode 28	41
Ode 29	43
Ode 30	44
Ode 31	44
Ode 32	46
Ode 34	47
Ode 35	48
Ode 36	48
Ode 37	49
Ode 39	51
Ode 40	52
Ode 41	53
Ode 42	54
Thank You for Reading	57

Preface - Message to the Reader

What If You Could Help Rebuild the Greatest Library in Human History?

Thousands of years ago, the Library of Alexandria stood as the crown jewel of human achievement — a sanctuary where the collected wisdom of every known civilization was gathered, preserved, and shared freely.

And then, it was lost.

Through fire, conquest, and the slow erosion of time, humanity lost not just books — but ideas, dreams, discoveries, and stories that could have changed the world forever.

Today, the Library of Alexandria lives again — and you are invited to be a part of its restoration.

Our mission is simple yet profound:

To rebuild the greatest library the world has ever known, and to translate all timeless works into every language and dialect, so that no seeker of knowledge is ever left behind again.

By joining our movement to rebuild the modern Library

of Alexandria, you become part of an unprecedented mission:

- **Unlimited Access to the Greatest Audiobooks & eBooks Ever Written:**

    Instantly explore thousands of legendary works—Plato, Shakespeare, Jane Austen, Leo Tolstoy, and countless more. All instantly available to read or listen, placing a complete literary universe at your fingertips.

- **Beautiful Paperback & Deluxe Editions at Printing Cost**

    Own any title as an elegant paperback, deluxe hardcover, or stunning collectible boxset—offered to you at true printing cost, delivered straight to your door. Build your personal Library of Alexandria, crafted for beauty, built for durability, and worthy of proud display.

- **Fresh Translations for Modern Readers—in Every Language & Dialect**

    Enjoy timeless masterpieces reimagined in clear, contemporary language—no more outdated phrases or obscure references. Alongside the original versions, we're tirelessly translating these classics into every language and dialect imaginable, ensuring accessibility and understanding across cultures and generations.

- **Join a Global Renaissance of Literature & Knowledge**

    You directly support expanding our library, publishing deluxe editions at true cost, translating works into all global languages, and bringing humanity's greatest stories to people everywhere. By joining today, you're not just preserving a legacy of masterpieces; you set in motion a powerful wave of literary accessibility.

Become a Torchbearer of Knowledge.

Join us for free now at **LibraryofAlexandria.com**

Together, we will ensure that the light of human wisdom never fades again.

With gratitude and a shared love of knowledge,

The Modern Library of Alexandria Team

Visit:

www.libraryofalexandria.com

Or scan the code below:

Introduction

The Voice of Devotion: A Sacred Songbook of Early Christian Faith

The Odes of Solomon stands as one of the most beautiful and spiritually evocative works to survive from the early centuries of Christianity. This collection of 42 ancient hymns, often referred to as the first Christian psalter, offers a glimpse into the devotional life of the earliest followers of Christ—a life shaped not by theological debate or institutional structure, but by the direct, joyful experience of divine love. These odes, attributed by tradition to King Solomon but more likely composed by an anonymous Christian mystic in the late first or early second century CE, speak with a voice of intimate connection to the Divine. They are personal, lyrical, deeply emotional, and unmistakably sacred.

Unlike the Psalms of the Hebrew Bible, which often oscillate between lament and praise, the Odes of Solomon are overwhelmingly filled with light, joy, gratitude, and spiritual triumph. They do not dwell on sin and repentance but lift the soul into the presence of the Divine, celebrating salvation, resurrection, spiritual renewal, and union with God. They reflect an early

Christian community steeped in mystical experience—a community for whom Christ was not only a teacher or savior, but the very embodiment of divine joy and eternal love.

In these hymns, we hear a soul that has been transformed by grace. The language of the odes is intensely personal—"I drank from the living water," "He lifted me up from the pit," "I was clothed with light"—and yet it speaks a universal message. The "I" in the poems is every soul that has known suffering and found healing in God. It is every person who has wandered in darkness and been brought into light. The Odes of Solomon do not aim to teach doctrine but to express an experience that transcends doctrine: the experience of being loved, known, and healed by the living God.

The poetic imagery in the odes is rich and varied. Water, light, breath, song, and fragrance are used not as literary flourishes but as manifestations of spiritual truth. The odes are filled with references to divine indwelling, sacred birth, heavenly light, and spiritual rebirth. These images flow one into another, blurring the boundaries between the physical and the spiritual, the historical and the eternal. The effect is one of immersion: the reader is drawn not into an argument, but into a song that echoes in the soul long after the words have ended.

Their theology is deeply incarnational and infused with the Spirit. Christ is not only the Savior who died and rose again—he is the living breath within the believer, the divine Word made manifest in the heart. The Spirit is ever-present, inspiring joy, granting speech, guiding the soul in truth. And God is never distant—he is the loving Father who embraces, nourishes, and abides. The Odes of Solomon are written from the vantage point of one who already knows this reality, and whose only response is to praise.

Transformation, Unity, and the Song of the New Creation

One of the most powerful aspects of The Odes of Solomon is their consistent theme of spiritual transformation. The speaker is not stagnant, but continually renewed. The odes describe a journey from silence to song, from weakness to strength, from sorrow to rejoicing. This is not merely metaphor—it is the lived experience of those who have passed through suffering and emerged into grace. This transformation is not self-willed; it is a gift from the Divine. Again and again, the odes speak of God's initiative—God lifts, God clothes, God breathes, God restores. The human response is to sing.

These hymns also reflect a powerful vision of unity. The soul is reunited with God, with others, and with its own divine purpose. Separation is overcome. Alienation is healed. This unity is not abstract—it is enacted in the body, the community, and the creation itself. The odes envision a new world in which all things are reconciled in love. There is no room for fear or hatred, because divine joy has filled all things. This eschatological vision is not postponed to some future age—it is already breaking into the present for those who live in the Spirit.

Many scholars note that the Odes of Solomon bear strong echoes of Gnostic and Jewish mystical thought, but they are not confined by any one tradition. They draw from the well of Hebrew prophecy, the beauty of Hellenistic lyricism, and the mystical Christ-centered devotion of early Christian spirituality. This synthesis creates a work that transcends boundaries, offering a truly universal expression of faith. The odes do not argue—they sing. They do not persuade—they illuminate. They speak not to the mind alone, but to the heart and the soul.

This modern translation seeks to preserve the lyrical power, emotional depth, and spiritual immediacy of the original text. Archaic phrasing has been softened, and poetic flow restored, without sacrificing the sacred rhythm and rich symbolism that define the odes. Each hymn has been treated not merely as a historical document, but as a living act of devotion—capable of touching the soul of the modern reader just as it inspired those who first sang them in secret gatherings, desert caves, or early house churches.

To read The Odes of Solomon is to encounter the sacred in its most intimate form. These are not only hymns to be admired—they are songs to be sung, prayers to be lived, truths to be embraced. They offer no instruction manual for the spiritual life—only the witness of a soul overflowing with love, gratitude, and joy. In an age of noise, they offer stillness. In a world of fragmentation, they offer wholeness. In a time of anxiety, they offer peace.

Let this book be a wellspring of renewal for your spirit. Let the odes become your own prayers, your own hymns, your own sacred breath. As you read, may you hear the voice of the one who sings in you, who lifts you, who fills you with light. May you come to know, through these ancient words, the eternal love that never ceases to call your name.

The Odes of Solomon

These songs are among the most beautiful expressions of peace and joy in the world today. However, their origins, the time they were written, and the exact meaning behind many of their verses remain a literary mystery.

The songs have survived in a single ancient manuscript written in Syriac, which seems to be a translation from the original Greek. Scholars have debated their history for years, and one of the most accepted theories is that they were created by newly baptized Christians in the First Century.

What sets these songs apart is that they do not reference historical events. They do not draw from the Old Testament or the Gospels, making their inspiration feel fresh and original. They echo the words of Aristides, who once described early Christians as "a new people with something Divine within them." The power and depth of these songs are comparable to the most moving passages of Scripture.

These remarkable and mysterious odes were translated for us by J. Rendel Harris, a well-respected scholar and Honorary Fellow of Clare College,

Cambridge. He describes them as works of extraordinary beauty and deep spiritual meaning, stating, "The only thing people seem to agree on is that the Odes are uniquely beautiful and hold great spiritual value."

Ode 1

> The Lord rests on my head like a crown, and He will never leave me.
> The crown of truth has been placed on me, and it has made Your branches grow within me.
> It is not a dry or lifeless crown that does not bloom.
> You live upon me, and through You, I have flourished.
> Your fruits are abundant and whole, filled with the salvation that comes from You.

Ode 2

[There is no extant copy of Ode 2]

Ode 3

I am wrapped in the love of the Lord.
His people are with Him, and I rely on them, just as He loves me.

I would not have known how to love the Lord if He had not first shown me His endless love.

Only someone who has been loved can truly understand love.

I love the One who loves me, and wherever He finds rest, I will be there too.

I will never feel like an outsider, because the Lord Most High is merciful and has no jealousy.

I am united with Him, for love has brought us together. Since I love the Son, I will also be called a child of God.

Anyone who is connected to the Eternal One will also share in eternal life.

Whoever finds joy in the Source of Life will also be filled with life.

This is the Spirit of the Lord, which is true and never deceives. It teaches people to understand His ways.

Be wise, gain understanding, and open your heart to His truth.

Hallelujah.

Ode 4

No one can change or take away Your holy place, O my God.
No one has power over it because You designed Your sanctuary long before creating sacred places.
What is ancient and holy cannot be changed by anything lesser. Lord, You have given Your heart to those who believe in You.
You are never still, and You always bring life and growth.
Just one moment of Your faithfulness is greater than all days and years combined.
Who can receive Your grace and then be rejected?
Your seal is known, and all Your creation recognizes it.
Your heavenly hosts carry it, and Your chosen archangels are clothed in it.
You have invited us to be with You, not because You need us, but because we always need You.
Pour out Your gentle rain upon us and open Your overflowing springs, filling us with all we need.
You never regret what You have promised, and nothing You say will ever change.
You knew the outcome from the very beginning.

What You have given, You have given freely, never to take it back.
Everything was clear and perfectly planned by You from the start.
Lord, You are the Creator of all things.
Hallelujah.

Ode 5

I praise You, Lord, because I love You.
O Most High, do not leave me, for You are my hope.
You have given me Your grace freely; may I live by it always.
My enemies may come after me, but do not let them find me.
Cover their eyes in darkness and surround them with thick shadows.
Let them have no light to guide them, so they cannot capture me.
Let their own plans trap them, so whatever they have plotted comes back on them.
They made their schemes, but they were never meant to succeed.
They prepared to harm me, but in the end, they were powerless.
My trust is in the Lord, and I will not be afraid.
Because the Lord is my salvation, I have nothing to fear.

He is like a crown upon my head, holding me steady.
Even if everything around me shakes, I will stand firm.
Even if all I see fades away, I will not be lost.
For the Lord is with me, and I am with Him.
Hallelujah.

Ode 6

Just as the wind moves through a harp and makes the strings play,
The Spirit of the Lord moves through me, and I speak with His love.
He removes everything that does not belong, for all things belong to the Lord.
This has been true from the beginning and will remain true forever.
Nothing can stand against Him, and nothing can rise above Him.
The Lord has spread His wisdom and wants His gifts to be known through His grace.
He gave us His praise for the sake of His name, and our spirits glorify His Holy Spirit.
A small stream began to flow and became a mighty, wide river, sweeping away everything in its path and leading to His Temple.
No walls built by people could stop it, nor could those skilled in controlling water hold it back.

It spread across the earth, filling everything in its way.
Then all who were thirsty drank deeply, and their thirst was satisfied.
For this drink was given by the Most High.
Blessed are those who serve this water, for they have been entrusted with His life-giving gift.
They refreshed dry lips and awakened weary hearts.
Even those close to death were revived by them.
They strengthened weak bodies and restored what had been broken.
They gave energy to the weary and brought light to fading eyes.
Everyone recognized them as belonging to the Lord, for they lived by His eternal, life-giving water.
Hallelujah.

Ode 7

Just as anger rises against evil, so does joy overflow for the Beloved, bringing blessings without limits.
My joy comes from the Lord, and my path leads to Him. This journey is beautiful.
I have a Helper—the Lord—who has revealed Himself to me with kindness and humility, making His greatness feel close.

He became like me so that I could receive Him. He took on my form so that I could welcome Him.

When I saw Him, I was not afraid, because He was full of grace toward me.

He made Himself like me so I could understand Him and see that He is near.

The Father of knowledge is the source of wisdom.

He who created wisdom is greater than anything He has made.

Before I even existed, He knew me and what I would do once I was born.

Because of this, He poured out His endless grace, allowing me to seek Him and receive the gift of His sacrifice.

He is perfect, unchanging, and the Creator of all worlds.

He has revealed Himself to those who belong to Him so they would recognize their Maker and understand that they did not create themselves.

He has opened the way to knowledge, making it wide, clear, and complete.

He has marked it with His light, stretching from the beginning to the end.

Everything serves Him, and the Son brings Him joy.

Through His salvation, He will claim all things as His own, and the Most High will be revealed to His holy ones.

They will proclaim His coming to those who sing of the Lord, so they may go out to meet Him with joy and music.

The prophets will go before Him, standing in His presence.

They will praise Him with love, for He is near and sees everything.

Hatred will disappear, and jealousy will be drowned.

Ignorance will be wiped away, for the knowledge of the Lord will fill the earth.

Let those who sing lift up the name of the Lord Most High and bring their songs of praise.

Let their hearts shine like daylight and their voices reflect the beauty of the Lord.

Let no one remain silent or without understanding.

For He gave every living being a voice to praise Him and declare His glory.

Let all speak of His power and share the goodness of His grace.

Hallelujah.

Ode 8

Open your hearts to the joy of the Lord, and let your love flow from within to your words.

Live a holy life, bearing good fruit for the Lord, and speak with wisdom in His light.

Rise up and stand tall, you who were once brought low.

You who were silent, speak now, for your mouth has been opened.

You who were once rejected, be lifted up, for your righteousness has been raised high.

The Lord's right hand is with you, and He will be your Helper.

Peace has been prepared for you, even before any battle you may face.

Listen to the word of truth and receive the wisdom of the Most High.

Your body may not understand what I am about to say, nor can your clothing reveal what I am about to show you.

Hold on to my mystery, you who are protected by it; hold on to my faith, you who are kept by it.

Understand my wisdom, you who truly know me; love me deeply, you who love.

I do not turn away from my own, for I know them.

Even before they existed, I saw them and placed my mark upon them.

I shaped their being and prepared my own nourishment for them, so they could drink from my holiness and live.

I take joy in them and am not ashamed of them.

They are my creation, made from my thoughts and purpose.
Who can stand against what I have made? Who can resist my will?
I created mind and heart, and they belong to me. I have placed my chosen ones in my right hand.
My righteousness goes before them, and they will never lose my name, for it remains with them.
Pray, grow, and remain in the love of the Lord.
You are loved in the Beloved, kept safe in the One who lives, and saved by the One who was saved.
You will remain unshaken for all generations because of the name of your Father.
Hallelujah.

Ode 9

Listen carefully, and I will speak to you.
Give yourself to me, so I may also give myself to you.
This is the word of the Lord and His plan—the holy purpose He has for His Messiah.
In the Lord's will, you find life; His purpose leads to eternal life, and His perfection never fades.
Be strengthened in God the Father, accept His plan, and stand firm, redeemed by His grace.
I bring you a message of peace, His holy ones, so that none who hear will fall in battle.

Those who know Him will not be lost, and those who receive Him will never feel ashamed.

Truth is an everlasting crown—blessed are those who wear it.

It is more precious than any jewel, for many battles have been fought over it.

But righteousness has claimed it and now offers it to you.

Wear this crown as a sign of your covenant with the Lord, and all who overcome will be written in His book.

For His book is the reward of victory, and it sees you before it, longing for you to be saved.

Hallelujah.

Ode 10

The Lord has guided my words with His truth and opened my heart with His light.

He has placed His eternal life within me and allowed me to share the blessings of His peace.

To help those who seek Him find new life and to lead those in bondage into freedom.

I found strength and courage, and I took hold of the world. What was once captivity became mine for the glory of the Most High, my God and Father.

Those who had been scattered were gathered together, but my love for them did not make me unclean, because they honored me in high places.

His light touched their hearts, and they followed my path, finding salvation. They became my people forever.

Hallelujah.

Ode 11

My heart was made clean, and its beauty bloomed. Then grace grew within me, and I produced good fruits for the Lord.

The Most High purified me with His Holy Spirit, opening my heart to Him and filling it with His love.

His cleansing became my salvation, and I walked in His path, in His peace, and in the way of truth.

From the beginning to the end, He gave me understanding.

He placed me on the rock of truth, making me strong where He had set me.

His refreshing waters touched my lips, flowing freely from the fountain of the Lord.

I drank deeply and was filled with joy from the living water that never runs dry.

This joy did not lead me to ignorance, but it made me turn away from worthless things.

I left behind empty pursuits and turned to the Most High, my God, gaining the riches of His blessings.

I rejected the foolishness of the world, threw it aside, and left it behind me.

The Lord gave me new garments and covered me in His light.

From above, He gave me eternal rest, and I became like a land full of life, blooming with joy.

The Lord shines upon me like the sun over the earth.

My eyes were opened, and my face was refreshed with His dew.

My breath was filled with the sweet fragrance of the Lord.

He brought me into His Paradise, where the treasures of His joy are stored.

I saw trees blooming and bearing fruit,

Their crowns growing naturally,

Their branches reaching upward, and their fruit shining brightly.

Their roots came from an everlasting land,

Watered by a river of joy,

Flowing through the land of eternal life.

Then I worshiped the Lord, amazed by His greatness.

I said, "Blessed are those, O Lord, who are planted in Your land and have a place in Your Paradise.

They grow like the trees You have planted, leaving darkness behind and stepping into light."

Look at all Your faithful workers—they are beautiful, doing what is right and turning away from evil to follow Your goodness.

The scent of every tree in Your land is changed, becoming sweet and pure.

Everything reflects You, Lord. Blessed are those who care for Your waters, and may Your faithful servants be remembered forever.

There is plenty of room in Your Paradise, and nothing is empty or barren—everything is full of fruit.

Glory to You, O God, the joy of Paradise forever.
Hallelujah.

Ode 12

He has filled me with words of truth so that I can speak about Him.

Just like water flows, truth flows from my mouth, and my lips share the good things He has done.

He has given me great knowledge because the Lord's words are true, and His light brings understanding.

The Most High has given Him to His people—

Those who explain His beauty,

Those who tell of His greatness,

Those who admit His plans,
Those who share His thoughts,
And those who teach about His works.
His words are beyond description, and just as He speaks with wisdom, He also moves with speed and sharpness, never slowing down.
He never falls but always stands firm, and no one can fully understand where He comes from or how He works.
Just as He does His work, He also brings hope, for He is the light that brings new ideas.
Through Him, generations spoke to one another, and even those who were silent found their voices.
Love and fairness came from Him, and people spoke to each other with kindness.
His words inspired them, and they came to know their Creator because they were united.
The Most High spoke to them, and His message spread because of Him.
The Word lives within people, and His truth is love.
Blessed are those who, through Him, understand all things and know the Lord in His truth.
Hallelujah.

Ode 13

Look! The Lord reflects who we are. Open your eyes and see yourself in Him.
Learn what you truly look like, and then praise His Spirit.
Wipe away anything that hides your true self, love His holiness, and make it a part of you.
Then, you will always remain pure with Him.
Hallelujah.

Ode 14

My eyes are always looking to You, Lord, just as a child looks to their father.
My joy and my heart belong to You.
Please don't turn away Your mercy, Lord, and never take Your kindness from me.
Reach out Your hand to me always, my Lord, and guide me to the end according to Your will.
Let me be pleasing to You because of Your greatness, and save me from evil for the sake of Your name.
Let Your gentleness stay with me, Lord, along with the blessings of Your love.
Teach me the songs of Your truth so I can grow and bear good fruit in You.

Open my heart to the music of Your Holy Spirit, so I can praise You with every note, Lord.
Show me Your mercy in abundance, and answer our prayers quickly.
For You are all we need.
Hallelujah.

Ode 15

Just as people rejoice when they see the sunrise, my joy comes from the Lord.
He is my Sun, and His light has lifted me up, driving away all darkness from my face.
Through Him, I have been given sight and have seen His holy day.
He has given me ears to hear His truth.
I have gained understanding and found great joy in Him.
I turned away from the wrong path, went toward Him, and received His abundant salvation.
Because of His kindness, He blessed me, and in His great beauty, He shaped me.
Through His name, I have put on eternal life, and by His grace, I have left behind all that fades away.
Death has disappeared before me, and the grave has lost its power because of His word.

Eternal life has begun in the Lord's kingdom, and it has been revealed to His faithful people, given freely to all who trust in Him.
Hallelujah.

Ode 16

Just as a farmer's work is with the plow, and a sailor's work is steering the ship, my work is singing to the Lord through His songs.
My passion and purpose are found in His hymns because His love has filled my heart, and He has placed His words on my lips.
The Lord is my greatest love, so I will sing to Him.
His praises give me strength, and I trust in Him completely.
When I open my mouth, His Spirit will speak through me, sharing the glory and beauty of the Lord—
The work of His hands, the detail of His creation,
The depth of His mercy, and the power of His Word.
For the Word of the Lord reveals what is unseen and makes His thoughts known.
Our eyes witness His creation, and our ears hear His wisdom.
He stretched out the land and placed the waters in the sea.

He spread out the sky and set the stars in place.
He shaped all of creation, set everything in motion, and then rested from His work.
All things follow their paths and fulfill their purpose, never stopping or failing.
Even the heavenly beings obey His Word.
The sun holds the light, and the night holds the darkness.
He made the sun to shine by day, and the night to bring darkness across the land.
Together, they reflect the beauty of God's design.
Nothing exists outside of the Lord, for He was here before anything began.
Everything was created by His Word and His wisdom.
Praise and honor to His name.
Hallelujah.

Ode 17

Then my God placed a crown on me, and it was full of life.
My Lord declared me righteous, for my salvation will never fade away.
I have been freed from empty pursuits, and I am no longer condemned.

He broke my chains with His own hands, gave me a new identity, and saved me as I walked with Him.

The truth guided my thoughts, and I followed it without losing my way.

Everyone who saw me was amazed, as if I were a stranger to them.

The One who truly knows me and lifts me up is the Most High, perfect in all things.

Through His kindness, He honored me and lifted my understanding to the highest truth.

From there, He showed me the path to follow, and I opened doors that had once been shut.

I broke through iron bars, for the chains that once held me had melted away.

Nothing was closed off to me, because He made me a way for all things to open.

I went to those who were still trapped so I could set them free, making sure no one remained in bondage.

I shared my knowledge freely, and through my love, I brought new life.

I planted my truth in people's hearts and changed them from within.

Then they received my blessing and truly lived, coming together and finding salvation.

They became part of me, and I became their leader.

Glory to You, our Head, O Lord Messiah.
Hallelujah.

Ode 18

My heart was lifted and filled with the love of the Most High so that I could praise Him with all that I am.
He gave me strength so I would not fall away from His power.
Sickness left my body, and I stood strong for the Lord because His kingdom will never be shaken.
Lord, for the sake of those in need, do not take Your Word away from me.
And do not hold back Your goodness because of what others do.
Let light never be defeated by darkness, and let truth never be chased away by lies.
Let Your mighty hand bring salvation to victory, gathering people from everywhere and protecting those who suffer.
You are my God—there is no falsehood or death in You; only perfection is in Your will.
You do not know what is empty and meaningless, because such things do not belong to You.
You are never mistaken, and mistakes cannot exist in You.

Foolishness appeared like dust in the wind, like foam on the sea.
Some people thought it was something great, but they became like it—empty and weak.
But those who understood saw the truth and did not let their minds be corrupted.
They stayed close to the thoughts of the Most High and saw the foolishness of those who had lost their way.
Then they spoke truth with the breath that the Most High had placed within them.
Praise and great honor to His name.
Hallelujah.

Ode 19

A cup of milk was given to me, and I drank it, tasting the sweetness of the Lord's kindness.
The Son is the cup, the Father is the one who provides the milk, and the Holy Spirit is the one who gathers it.
His blessings were overflowing, and it was meant to be shared, not wasted.
The Holy Spirit poured out this gift, blending the richness of the Father's love.
She gave it to the world without them realizing, and those who received it were made whole by His power.

The Virgin's womb took it in, and she conceived and gave birth.
She became a mother, filled with deep mercy.
She gave birth without pain because it was all part of a greater purpose.
She needed no midwife, for He Himself brought life through her.
With strength and great desire, she delivered Him, fulfilling what was promised by God's power.
She embraced Him with love, protected Him with kindness, and declared His glory.
Hallelujah.

Ode 20

I am a priest of the Lord, and I serve Him faithfully.
To Him, I offer the sacrifice of His own wisdom.
For His wisdom is not like the world's, not like the flesh, nor like those who worship in a worldly way.
The Lord desires offerings of righteousness, a pure heart, and truthful words.
Give yourself to Him with honesty, and do not let your kindness be a burden to others, nor treat others unfairly.
Do not take advantage of a stranger, for they are like you. Do not deceive your neighbor or take away what they need.

Instead, clothe yourself in the Lord's grace and enter His paradise. Take from His tree and make for yourself a crown.

Wear it with joy, rest in His presence, and be at peace.

His glory will go before you, and you will receive His kindness and grace. You will be anointed in truth and sing praises to His holiness.

Praise and honor to His name.

Hallelujah.

Ode 21

I lifted my arms high because of the Lord's kindness.

He broke my chains and set me free. My Helper lifted me up with His mercy and salvation.

I left behind the darkness and stepped into the light.

He made me whole, and my body was free from pain, sickness, or suffering.

The Lord's wisdom guided me, and His presence was always with me.

He lifted me into the light, and I stood before Him.

I stayed close to Him, always praising and thanking Him.

He filled my heart so much that His praise overflowed from my mouth and onto my lips.

Then my face shined with joy, celebrating the Lord and His goodness.

Hallelujah.

Ode 22

He brought me down from above and lifted me up from below.

He gathers what is in between and hands it over to me.

He scattered my enemies and those who stood against me.

He gave me the power to break chains so I could set others free.

Through me, He defeated the seven-headed dragon and placed me at its roots so I could destroy its offspring.

You were always with me, guiding me, and Your name surrounded me everywhere I went.

Your mighty hand wiped out its poisonous evil and cleared the path for those who believe in You.

You called people out of their graves and separated them from the dead.

You took dry bones and covered them with flesh.

But they remained still, so You filled them with the breath of life.

Your ways and Your presence never change. You allowed the world to decay so that everything could be restored and made new.

The foundation of all things is built upon You, the solid rock. Upon it, You have built Your kingdom, a home for those who are holy.
Hallelujah.

Ode 23

Joy belongs to those who are holy. Who else can truly receive it but them?
Grace is given to those chosen by God. And who can accept it except those who have trusted in it from the very beginning?
Love is for those whom God has set apart. And who can embrace it but those who have carried it in their hearts from the start?
Walk in the wisdom of the Lord, and you will experience His grace in abundance—both for His glory and the fullness of His truth.
His wisdom was like a letter sent down from above,
Shot like an arrow from a powerful bow.
Many hands reached out, trying to grab it, hoping to take hold and read it.
But it slipped through their fingers, and they feared both the letter and the seal upon it.
They could not break the seal, for the power behind it was greater than them.

Still, some followed after it, wanting to know where it would land, who would read it, and who would hear its message.

Then a great wheel caught the letter and carried it forward.

With it came a sign of the kingdom and God's plan.

Everything that stood in its way was cleared out and removed.

It silenced many enemies and made a way where there was none.

It crossed over rivers, tore down forests, and created a clear path.

The head bowed down to the feet, for the wheel moved beneath them, carrying everything along with it.

The letter carried a command, and all the nations gathered together.

At its head was the One who was revealed—the Son of Truth, sent from the Most High Father.

He took possession of all things, and the plans of those who opposed Him came to nothing.

Those who tried to deceive others became weak and fled, and those who persecuted Him vanished.

Then the letter became a great book, completely written by the hand of God.

The name of the Father was upon it, along with the Son and the Holy Spirit, to reign forever and ever.
Hallelujah.

Ode 24

The dove fluttered above the head of our Lord Messiah because He was her leader.
She sang over Him, and her voice was heard.
The people were afraid, and strangers were unsettled.
The bird took flight, and every small creature hid away.
Deep places opened and closed, as if searching for the Lord like a mother about to give birth.
But He was not given to them as food, for He did not belong to them.
Instead, the deep places were sealed by the Lord, and they disappeared along with their old ways of thinking.
They had struggled from the beginning, but their struggle led to life.
Yet those who were lacking perished because they could not hold on to the truth.
The Lord destroyed the plans of those who did not have truth in them.

They lacked wisdom, even though they thought
    highly of themselves.
So they were cast aside, for they did not have the
    truth.
But the Lord made His way clear and poured out
    His grace for all to see.
And those who understood recognized His holiness.
Hallelujah.

Ode 25

You set me free from my chains, and I ran to You,
    my God.
You are the hand that saves me and my Helper in
    times of need.
You stopped those who rose against me, and they
    disappeared.
Because Your presence was with me, and Your
    grace saved me.
But many looked down on me and rejected me,
    treating me like something worthless.
Yet You gave me strength and helped me.
You placed a lamp on both my right and left, filling
    me with light so that no darkness remained in
    me.
Your Spirit covered me, and I left behind my old
    self.

Your mighty hand lifted me up and took away my sickness.
I became strong in Your truth and holy in Your righteousness.
All my enemies feared me, and I belonged fully to the Lord.
Your kindness made me right with You, and Your peace lasts forever.
Hallelujah.

Ode 26

I lifted my voice in praise to the Lord because I belong to Him.
I will sing His holy song because my heart is with Him.
His harp is in my hands, and His songs of peace will never be silenced.
With all my heart, I will call to Him, praising and honoring Him with everything in me.
From the East to the West, His name is praised.
From the South to the North, He is thanked.
From the highest peaks to the farthest ends, His greatness is seen.
Who can write the songs of the Lord, or who can truly understand them?
Who can prepare himself for eternal life and save himself?

Who can reach the Most High and make Him speak?
Who can explain the wonders of the Lord? Even if the one who tries is gone, what he spoke of will remain.
It is enough to understand and be fulfilled, for those who sing for the Lord stand in perfect peace—
Like a river flowing from a powerful spring, bringing refreshment to those who seek it.
Hallelujah.

Ode 27

I lifted my hands and honored my Lord,
For stretching out my hands is a sign of Him.
And my outstretched arms form the shape of the cross.
Hallelujah.

Ode 28

The Spirit surrounds my heart like a mother dove covering her young, feeding them with care.
My heart is always renewed and filled with joy, like a baby leaping in its mother's womb.
I trusted in Him, and so I found peace, because the One I trust is always faithful.
He has blessed me greatly, and I am with Him.

No weapon can separate me from Him—not a dagger, not a sword.

I am prepared before trouble comes, standing on His side, which never dies.

Eternal life has embraced me and filled me with love.

The Spirit within me comes from that life, and it cannot die, because it is life itself.

People were shocked when they saw me suffering.

They thought I was defeated, like someone who was lost forever.

But what seemed like my downfall became my salvation.

They rejected me because I had no jealousy in my heart.

I was hated for constantly doing good.

They attacked me like wild dogs, foolishly turning against the One who cared for them.

Their thoughts were twisted, and their hearts were full of confusion.

But I carried water in my right hand, and I met their bitterness with kindness.

I did not fall because I was not like them, and I was not born from the same place as they were.

They wanted to destroy me, but they couldn't, because I existed before their time, and their plans against me were useless.

Even those who tried to erase the memory of the One before them failed.

For the wisdom of the Most High cannot be controlled, and His ways are greater than all understanding.

Hallelujah.

Ode 29

The Lord is my hope, and I will never be ashamed of trusting in Him.

He created me to bring Him praise, and in His kindness, He has blessed me.

By His mercy, He lifted me up, and through His great honor, He raised me high.

He brought me out of the depths of death and saved me from its grasp.

He helped me defeat my enemies and made me right through His grace.

I put my faith in the Lord's Messiah and knew that He is the Lord.

He showed me His sign and guided me with His light.

He gave me His power so I could stand against the plans of the wicked and humble the strength of the powerful.

By His Word, I fought the battle and won the victory through His might.

The Lord crushed my enemy with His Word, scattering him like dust in the wind.
So I give praise to the Most High, for He has honored His servant and the son of His faithful one.
Hallelujah.

Ode 30

Come and take water from the Lord's living fountain—it has been opened for you.
All who are thirsty, come and drink. Rest beside the Lord's fountain.
Its water is pure, sparkling, and always refreshing.
It is sweeter than honey, and no honeycomb can compare.
For it flows from the Lord's lips and comes straight from His heart.
It came without limits, unseen, and many did not recognize it until it was placed before them.
Blessed are those who drink from it and are renewed.
Hallelujah.

Ode 31

Deep valleys disappeared before the Lord, and darkness faded when He appeared.

Lies collapsed and were destroyed by Him, and arrogance had no place because the truth of the Lord overcame it.

He opened His mouth and spoke words of grace and joy, singing a new song to His name.

Then He lifted His voice to the Most High and presented to Him those who became His children through Him.

His face shined with righteousness, just as His Holy Father had intended.

Come, all who are suffering, and receive joy.

Take hold of His grace and accept the gift of eternal life.

They judged me even though I had done no wrong.

They took what was mine, even though they had no right to it.

But I stayed calm and silent, refusing to be shaken by them.

I stood firm, like a strong rock that is struck again and again by crashing waves but does not move.

I endured their cruelty with humility so that I could save my people and guide them.

I did this to keep the promises made to the ancestors, for I was sent to bring salvation to their descendants.

Hallelujah.

Ode 32

Joy fills the hearts of those who are blessed, and
    light comes from the One who lives within them.
The Word of truth exists by itself,
For it is strengthened by the Holy Power of the
    Most High and will never be shaken.
Hallelujah.
Ode 33
But grace moved quickly and cast out the Deceiver,
    coming down to reject him.
He brought destruction before him and ruined
    everything he had done.
He stood on the highest peak and shouted from one
    end of the earth to the other.
He gathered all who followed him, because he did
    not appear as the Evil One.
But the pure and faithful one stood firm, calling out
    and saying:
"O sons of men, turn back! And you, daughters,
    come to me.
Leave the path of the Deceiver and follow me
    instead.
I will come into your lives, rescue you from
    destruction, and teach you the ways of truth.
Do not let yourselves be ruined or lost.

Listen to me and be saved, for I bring you the grace
   of God.
Through me, you will be saved and find blessing. I
   am your judge.
Those who follow me will not be falsely accused but
   will live forever in the new world.
My chosen ones walk with me, and I will show my
   ways to those who seek me. I will give them my
   name as a promise."
Hallelujah.

Ode 34

There is no struggle for those with a pure heart, and
   no obstacle for those who think rightly.
A clear mind is not shaken by chaos.
When someone is surrounded by goodness, they
   remain whole and at peace.
What is above reflects what is below.
For everything comes from above, and what seems
   to come from below only appears real to those
   who lack understanding.
Grace has been revealed to save you. Believe, live,
   and be saved.
Hallelujah.

Ode 35

The gentle rain of the Lord covered me with peace, and a cloud of calmness rose above my head.
It stayed with me, protecting me at all times, and became my salvation.
People around me were troubled and afraid, and from them came anger and judgment.
But I remained at peace in the Lord's presence—He was my shelter, stronger than any foundation.
He carried me like a mother carries her child and nourished me with the Lord's kindness.
His favor filled my life, and I found rest in His perfection.
I lifted my hands and turned my heart toward the Most High, and He saved me.
Hallelujah.

Ode 36

I rested in the Spirit of the Lord, and She lifted me up to heaven.
She set me on my feet in the Lord's high place, before His greatness and glory, where I praised Him with songs.
The Spirit brought me into the presence of the Lord, and because I was the Son of Man, I was called the Light, the Son of God.

I was honored above all the honored ones and made greater than the great ones.

For just as the Most High is great, He made me great, and just as He is always new, He renewed me.

He anointed me with His perfection, and I became one of those close to Him.

My words poured out like refreshing dew, and my heart overflowed with righteousness.

I walked in peace and was strengthened by the Spirit of God's care.

Hallelujah.

Ode 37

I lifted my hands to the Lord and raised my voice to the Most High.

I spoke from deep within my heart, and He heard me when my words reached Him.

His Word came to me, bringing the reward for my efforts.

And He gave me rest through His grace.

Hallelujah.

Ode 38

I entered the light of Truth as if riding in a chariot, and the Truth guided me forward.

It led me safely over deep valleys and dangerous cliffs, protecting me from harm.

It became my place of safety and set me on the path to eternal life.

He walked with me, gave me rest, and kept me from going the wrong way because He is and always will be the Truth.

I was never in danger because I stayed close to Him, and I never lost my way because I followed His voice.

For deception runs from Him and never crosses His path.

But Truth moves straight ahead, showing me what I did not understand—

Revealing the lies that poison the mind and the pain that disguises itself as pleasure.

I saw the corruption of the Deceiver, how he dressed up falsehood to look beautiful, pretending to be a bridegroom with a bride.

I asked the Truth, "Who are they?" And He answered, "This is the Deceiver and the Lie."

"They try to imitate the Beloved and His Bride, leading the world astray and filling it with corruption."

"They invite many to their false wedding feast and give them wine that clouds their minds."

"They make people forget their wisdom and throw away their knowledge, replacing it with foolishness."

"Then they abandon them, leaving them lost, wandering like people without direction."

"They do not seek understanding because they have none."

But I was made wise so that I would not fall into the hands of the Deceivers, and I rejoiced because the Truth was with me.

I was made strong, I lived, and I was saved, for the Lord's hand had laid my foundation.

He planted me, setting my roots deep, watering and blessing me so that my fruit would last forever.

I grew strong, spreading out and thriving.

And the Lord alone was glorified—

In His planting, His care, and His blessing.

In the beauty of His work and the wisdom of His plan.

Hallelujah.

Ode 39

The powerful rivers of the Lord rush forward, sweeping away those who reject Him.

They block their paths, destroy their crossings,

Pull them under, and ruin them completely.

These waters move faster than lightning, even more swiftly than the wind.

But those who cross with faith will not be harmed.

Those who walk on them with trust will not be shaken.

Because the Lord's mark is on these waters, and His sign is the path for those who cross in His name.

So take on the name of the Most High and know Him, and you will pass through safely, for the rivers will obey you.

The Lord has made a way across them with His Word—He walked on them and crossed on foot.

His footsteps stayed firm on the waters and did not disappear; they are like a strong bridge built on truth.

Waves rose high on both sides, but the steps of our Lord Messiah remained steady.

They were never washed away or destroyed.

And this path has been prepared for those who follow after Him—those who stay true to His faith and worship His name.

Hallelujah.

Ode 40

Just as honey drips from a honeycomb and milk flows from a mother to her child, so my hope flows to You, O my God.

Like a fountain pouring out water, my heart overflows with praise for the Lord, and my lips speak His glory.

His songs make my tongue sweet, and His music fills my whole being.

My face shines with joy in His presence, my spirit celebrates His love, and my soul glows in Him.

Those who are afraid can put their trust in Him, for He brings sure salvation.

He gives the gift of eternal life, and those who receive it will never be destroyed.

Hallelujah.

Ode 41

Let all of God's children praise Him, and let us accept the truth of His faith.

His people are known by Him, so let us sing with joy because of His love.

We have life through the Lord's grace, and we receive it through His Messiah.

A great light has shined on us, and the One who shares His glory with us is truly wonderful.

So let us all come together in the name of the Lord and honor Him for His goodness.

Let our faces shine in His light, and may our hearts reflect on His love, day and night.

Let us celebrate with the joy of the Lord.

People who see me will be amazed because I am different from them.

For the Father of Truth remembered me—the One who has known me from the beginning.

His riches brought me into being, formed from the thoughts of His heart.

His Word is with us wherever we go—our Savior, who gives life and never rejects us.

He humbled Himself but was lifted up because of His righteousness.

The Son of the Most High appeared, reflecting the perfection of His Father.

Light shined from the Word, which existed before time began.

The Messiah is the one true Savior. He was known before the world was created so that He could bring eternal life through the power of His name.

A new song of praise belongs to the Lord from those who love Him.

Hallelujah.

Ode 42

I lifted my hands and reached out to my Lord, for stretching out my hands is a sign of Him.

My arms formed the shape of the upright cross, the same cross that was raised for the Righteous One.

I became invisible to those who never truly knew me, for I will not show myself to those who do not belong to me.
But I will be with those who love me.
All who persecuted me have perished. They searched for me, those who spoke against me, because I am alive.
Then I rose and stood with my people, speaking through their voices.
For they have turned away from their persecutors, and I covered them with the love that binds them to me.
Like a bridegroom holding his bride, so is my love upon those who know me.
And just as a bridal chamber is prepared for the wedding, my love surrounds those who believe in me.
Though I was rejected, I did not truly fall, and though they thought I was gone, I did not perish.
The grave saw me and was shattered, and death released me along with many others.
I became bitterness to death, sinking deep into its depths.
But it could not hold me—its power was broken, and it let go of my hands and feet because it could not withstand my presence.

Among the dead, I created a gathering of the living.
 I spoke to them with words full of life, so that
 my message would not be wasted.
Those who had died ran toward me, crying out:
"Son of God, have mercy on us!
Show us Your kindness and set us free from the
 chains of darkness.
Open the door so we may come to You, for now we
 see that death has no power over You.
Save us as well, for You are our Savior!"
I heard their cries and held their faith in my heart.
Then I placed my name upon their heads, for they
 were now free, and they belong to me.
Hallelujah.

Thank You for Reading

Dear Reader,

We hope this timeless classic has sparked your imagination and enriched your literary journey. Now that you've turned the final page, we want to share a vision for the future of reading—one where every classic you've ever wanted to explore is at your fingertips, in a format that best suits your life.

We'd like to invite you to gain immediate, unlimited digital & audiobook access to hundreds of the most treasured literary classics ever written—along with the option to secure deluxe paperback, hardcover & box set editions at printing cost. Together, we can spark a new global literary renaissance alongside our small, independent publishing house called "The Library of Alexandria."

Thousands of years ago, the Library of Alexandria stood as a beacon of knowledge—until it was lost to history. We aim to reignite that spirit of preservation and discovery right now, in the modern age—only this time, it's accessible to all, in every language and every format.

Picture a world where every timeless classic, novel, poem, or philosophical treatise is not only available to read but also updated for today's readers—modernized, translated into any language or dialect, and ready to enjoy in any format you choose, whether that is in an eBook, audiobook, paperback, or deluxe hardcover & box set version a printing cost.

By joining our movement to rebuild the modern Library of Alexandria, you become part of an unprecedented mission to offer:

- **Unlimited Audiobook & eBook Access to the Greatest Classics of All Time**

    Instantly explore thousands of legendary works, from Plato and Shakespeare to Jane Austen and Leo Tolstoy. All are instantly ready to read or listen to, giving you a complete literary universe at your fingertips.

- **Paperback & Deluxe Editions at Printing Costs:**

    Purchase any title in a paperback, deluxe hardbound, or deluxe boxset edition at printing costs, shipped right to your doorstep. Curate your personal library of Alexandria with editions worthy of display—crafted to last, designed to captivate, and delivered straight to your door.

- **Modern translations for Contemporary Readers in all languages and dialects**

  Discover a vast selection of classics reimagined in clear, current language—no more struggling with outdated phrases or obscure references. Next to the original versions, we aim to offer translations in as many languages and dialects as possible.

  As we continue our translation efforts and add new languages, readers everywhere can connect with these works as if they were written today. By bridging linguistic divides, you're contributing to ensuring that these timeless stories become more meaningful, accessible, and inspiring for people across the globe.

- **Your Personal Library of Alexandria:**

  Over the months and years, you'll curate a unique physical archive of classics—each volume a testament to your taste, curiosity, and love of knowledge. It's not just about owning books—it's about curating a cultural legacy you'll cherish and pass down for generations to come.

- **Join a Global Literary Renaissance:**

  Your support fuels an ongoing mission: allowing us to reinvest in offering deluxe print editions (including special boxsets) at their true cost, broaden the range of available formats and translations, and extend the reach of these works to new audiences worldwide. By joining today, you're not just preserving a legacy of masterpieces; you set in motion a powerful wave of literary accessibility.

We are more than a publisher—we're a movement, and we can't do it alone. Your support lets us scale our mission, preserving and reimagining history's greatest works for tomorrow's readers.

Become a Torchbearer of knowledge.

Thank you for picking up this book and allowing us into your literary journey. As you turn the pages, know that you're part of something larger: a global effort to keep these stories alive, share their wisdom across borders and generations, and spark a true cultural revival for the modern era.

If this resonates with you—please consider taking the next step by visiting:

www.libraryofalexandria.com

With gratitude and a shared love of knowledge,

The Modern Library of Alexandria Team

Visit:

www.libraryofalexandria.com

Or scan the code below:

www.ingramcontent.com/pod-product-compliance
Lightning Source LLC
LaVergne TN
LVHW030631080426
835512LV00021B/3455